Blessings in Disguise

The Insight Series

CONCORDIA PUBLISHING HOUSE · SAINT LOUIS

Edited by Robert C. Baker

Scripture quotations are from The Holy Bible, English Standard Version®. Copyright © 2001 by Crossway Bibles, a publishing ministry of Good News Publishers, Wheaton, Illinois. Used by permission. All rights reserved.

Hymn texts with the abbreviation *LSB* are from *Lutheran Service Book*, copyright © 2006 by Concordia Publishing House. All rights reserved.

Prayers are taken from *The Lord Will Answer: A Daily Prayer Catechism*. Copyright © 2004 by Concordia Publishing House. All rights reserved.

This publication may be available in braille, in large print, or on cassette tape for the visually impaired. Please allow 8 to 12 weeks for delivery. Write to Lutheran Blind Mission, 7550 Watson Rd., St. Louis, MO 63119-4409; call toll-free 1-888-215-2455; or visit the Web site: www.blindmission.org.

Manufactured in the United States of America

1 2 3 4 5 6 7 8 9 10   17 16 15 14 13 12 11 10 09 08

Contents

Hymnal Key
LSB = Lutheran Service Book
ELH = Evangelical Lutheran Hymnary
CW = Christian Worship
LW = Lutheran Worship
LBW = Lutheran Book of Worship
TLH = The Lutheran Hymnal

About This Series

This course is one of the Insight Series of short (four-session) adult Bible study courses, each looking at an important biblical topic or theme. Using these courses, you will gain insight into a portion of the Scriptures as you hear what God is saying to you there about Himself, about you, and about His Good News of salvation in Jesus Christ. These insights will help you as you go about your disciple's task of living in the Word and will equip you for a more fruitful study of the Word on your own in the future.

Using This Course

This course is designed to be used for small-group discussions. Each of the four sixty- to ninety-minute sessions you will find in this booklet will provide you with a clear picture of where the session is going and what it is supposed to accomplish, give you a way to lead into the session's study, provide input and discussion questions to guide your study of the text, suggest ways to follow up on the study during the week, and offer closing worship aids.

You will not need a teacher for this course. The printed material will guide you through the study. No one will have to be the answerer. But you will get the most from these materials if you:

1. Assign a leader for each session. That person should:

   a. Make sure he or she works through the material before the session and, if possible, looks at some additional resources to enrich your study.

   b. Begin and end the session with worship. The devotional time may be quite brief; a prayer or a Bible reading is sufficient. You might assign the opening and closing to a worship leader for each session.

   c. Keep the discussion moving. There is a tendency to get bogged down on some questions. The leader should be willing to say, "We'd better move on to the next point."

d. Make some choices if time is limited. The leader will want to select those items from the session's content that seem to be most helpful if it is clear there will not be time to work through all of the material.

e. Listen. Make sure everyone is heard. Give each a chance to speak. Encourage participation.

f. Pray for all participants.

2. Prepare for each session. The discussion will work better, the material will be more meaningful, and the Word will speak more clearly if everyone in the class works through the session's material before the class session. Even if preparation is limited to reading through the texts that will be a part of the session's study, the effort will enrich your study.

3. Meet regularly (at least once a week) in a convenient and comfortable place. Too much time between sessions means that learning will be forgotten and much time will be used in constant review. Too little time between sessions does not allow time for you to connect what you have learned to your daily living.

4. Provide resources. Preparation that includes a chance to look at commentaries, Bible dictionaries, Bible reference books, maps, and so on will add to your class. Encourage those who do such research to contribute what they have learned or discovered as you study.

5. Encourage participation. The course offers many opportunities to discuss biblical texts and to talk about application of the Word to each individual's life. The key is sharing. Everyone should have a chance to listen and to be heard. The goal is encouragement. We want to build one another up as we study the Word. We want to share the hope and the strength we receive by the power of the Spirit through that Word. We want to allow each person to come closer to the Savior as he or she encounters Him in the Word. Emphasize the positive. Share the joy of the Gospel. Celebrate His promised presence as "two or three" gather in His name.

Participant Introduction

Although Jesus' Sermon on the Mount (Matthew 5–7) is well known, His Sermon on the Plain (Luke 6) packs a powerful message too. Not as well known, this sermon of Jesus is just as challenging to Jesus' followers and every bit as comforting.

Unique to our Lord's sermon in Luke, His four beatitudes ("blessings") are paired with four jolting condemnations ("woes"). The four sessions of this Insight course follow this built-in outline. Used as a tool to dig into Scripture itself, this course can help today's Christian find Christ's power and encouragement in His Word, especially at times when the cross of discipleship grows heavy and is full of splinters.

∽ Session 1 ∾

Blessed the Poor/ Woe to the Rich

Our Goals for This Session

By the power of the Spirit working through God's Word, we want to

- explore what our Lord means by "rich" and "poor," and how we can apply those terms to ourselves;
- allow the Spirit to examine our hearts through the Word so we will see what our true riches are; and
- find the strength, comfort, and joy that our Lord gives the "poor" who, out of faith, follow Him.

Getting Started

Ask two members of your group to read the parts of Ronald and Julie:

Ronald: When did I change? Well, it didn't happen overnight. It took years of watching my father working, sweating, stewing, just to make ends meet. And watching my mother either paying bills or complaining about them. Dad always said, "Money's not the most important thing in life." But it was. Over supper that's all my folks talked about, fretted and fought about—until we turned on the TV or went to bed. We never had enough money. And I vowed that I'd never be like that!

Julie: But you're doing the same thing, Ron. You're as eaten up by money as they ever were. Ever since you got the new job, you've plunged into it as though nothing else in life was important. You're just like your parents.

Ronald: Oh, but I'm different. You see, my folks only pretended that money wasn't important. But I'm not going to pretend. It is important. I want it. And I don't see why I should let anything stand in my way to keep me from getting more of it.

Julie: Even Christ? Even if He has something to say about it? But you haven't been around to hear Him, Ron.

Ronald: There you go again, Julie. Just because I quit going to church doesn't mean I gave up God. It's just that I don't buy this business of giving up everything to be a Christian. Why, you'd think God wanted us all to be beggars.

Julie: But we are, Ron. We are. And all Christ wants of us is simply to admit it.

As a young, recently engaged couple, Ronald and Julie have been trying to lay some foundations for their future life together. However, some trouble spots are developing.

1. What problems do you see in their relationship to each other? in their relationship to Christ?

2. Ronald insists he is not like his parents. What evidence does he give to show that he's different? What reason(s) does Julie give to show she disagrees with Ronald? With whom do you agree, and why?

3. Ronald obviously feels that he grew up in a poor home because his family "never had enough money." Why or why

not do you think that Jesus' words "Blessed are you who are poor" (Luke 6:20b) apply to him?

4. Ronald feels that Christianity calls him to give up everything, that God wants us to be beggars. How is Ronald correct in his estimation of Christianity? How is he wrong? What insight do you believe Julie has with her last comment that we are beggars? Do you think Ronald will be willing to accept Julie's statement? Why or why not?

Defining "Poor," Defining "Rich"

First Step

Read Luke 6:20, 24. The poor are blessed? The rich are under woe? Obviously, this is not the way the world looks at being rich or being poor. Jesus must see something hidden from the world, but He doesn't want it hidden from us.

5. It would be stretching the point to consider all of Jesus' disciples as materially poor. Therefore, are Jesus' wealthier disciples excluded from His kingdom and those who are materially poor included? Give reasons for your answer. What is the basis for entrance into the Kingdom?

6. "Poor in spirit" is how Jesus clarifies His meaning (see Matthew 5:3). "Poor" here describes the attitude and condition of the heart, mind, and soul before God. If you were "poor" in

this sense, you would see only your need before God. So why does Jesus call this state "blessed"?

Second Step

7. Jesus points out, nevertheless, that a person materially well off is less likely to be spiritually "poor."

a. Jesus' remark about the wealthy person's possible entrance into the kingdom of God is stunning, and was meant to be (see Luke 18:24–25). In your own words, explain why the materially well off find it harder to enter the kingdom of God (v. 24)?

b. Why is it more difficult to sense our need for God, His grace, His forgiveness, if we are financially well off?

8. Hard! Not impossible, however. The "eye of a needle" to which Jesus referred may possibly have meant the small entrance at the base of a narrow tower, rather than a sewing needle. Camels could enter but had a reputation for stubbornly refusing to lower their heads, therefore blocking their own entrance. How is that like us, if we are contented with ourselves?

Rich Man, Poor Man, Beggar Man . . .

One classic contrast between the self-satisfied person and the poor-in-spirit person is seen in Jesus' parable of the rich man and Lazarus. Read Luke 16:19–31 briefly, then discuss:

9. Rich man: He had it all (v. 19). He was everything we might like to be: self-contained, secure, wanting for nothing, needing no one.

a. Jesus' hearers may not have been as well off as the rich man but they wanted to be! Could we be materially poor but still be like the rich man? Explain your answer.

b. It is not money itself but loving it that is a root of all evils. Read 1 Timothy 6:10. Explain how loving money can make it into a substitute (and false) god. How was Ronald (in the introduction to this lesson) wandering from faith in Christ to faith in money?

c. Greed can become like a drug. How does that truth explain why Jesus so utterly condemned this desire in His disciples (Luke 6:24)? What can such striving after money and power do to ourselves as His people? What does it do to the Church's mission and ministry?

d. Especially chilling, then, is Jesus' pronouncement that the rich man has already received his comfort (v. 24). Considering who "the Comforter" is, how have "lovers of money" exiled themselves from the best comfort?

10. Poor man: According to the Greek of the New Testament, the word for "poor" can mean "beggar" (v. 20), someone even lower than a "poor man." The very same word is used in the beatitude (Luke 6:20), so that we hear Jesus saying, "Blessed beggars"!

a. Lazarus had nothing—nothing physical or spiritual. Share only if you wish to: Have you ever felt like Lazarus—that you had nothing to offer God? nothing to attract His attention? What was that experience like?

b. Actually, the rich man had nothing more going for him than Lazarus did. He only thought he did. At the end of the parable, when Jesus revealed reality, which man was begging (Luke 16:22–26)? and which man was "comforted" (v. 25)? How do you explain this switch?

c. Beggars have nothing and need everything. Why can that realization be a head start in meeting our Savior?

d. For beggars Christ Jesus is the only Way to go; they have nothing else. They are the poor He blesses. How does

Christ Jesus bless beggars? (Read the Magnificat of Mary in Luke 1:46–55, especially vv. 46–48 and 51–53.) How does this blessing from Christ touch you? How has Christ Jesus specifically blessed you?

For Yours Is the Kingdom of God—but When?

The promise is clear if stunning. Poor beggars are blessed! They have the kingdom of God.

Yet all too often we tend to "futurize" all of Christ's promises. We think, "Oh, yes, someday when I'm in heaven, then (and only then!) I'll be blessed." We sometimes imagine that poor beggarman Lazarus also had to wait for his blessings.

Share with each other: Why is this is a commonly held view among Christians? among your group? What scriptural evidence is there that all our blessings are on hold, in heaven only?

Closely reread Jesus' statement in Luke 6:20 about the kingdom of God.

11. What tense (past, present, or future) does the Gospel use? What does that mean as to when we beggars have the kingdom of God? Do we have to wait to be included?

12. Some say that "heaven can wait." Oh, no it can't! The kingdom of heaven goes where the King goes, and King Jesus comes to beggars now by Word and Sacrament. By grace, they have now what later they will see face-to-face. As His beggars, what "hints of heaven" has Christ already given you?

In Conclusion

Beggars are blessed! Theirs is the kingdom of God!

Although we may not always feel blessed, it's comforting to know that God loves and blesses us, whether or not we feel it. No longer do we need to look to outward wealth, nor inward goodness, as evidence of God's love. Even in the pits of poverty (spiritual or physical), Christ Jesus comes with His grace.

Before you leave, share your favorite New Testament report of Jesus being with (and thus blessing) beggars. Note that not all beggars were physically poor. One example may be Nicodemus, in John 3. Another might be Ronald (see the introduction to this session). Share how the New Testament episode you picked strengthens and comforts you.

In Closing

In your closing prayer, be sure to include the petition "Thy kingdom come." Pray for vision to see how you, a beggar, can show other beggars how the King comes to beggars, such as to your congregation!

Prayer: May our Lord Jesus Christ Himself and God our Father, who loves us and by His grace gives us eternal encouragement and good hope, encourage our hearts and strengthen us in every good deed and word. Amen. (From 2 Thessalonians 2:16–17)

Close by singing or reading in unison "My Faith Looks Up to Thee" (*LSB* 702; *ELH* 184; *CW* 402; *LW* 378; *LBW* 479; *TLH* 394).

My faith looks up to Thee,
Thou Lamb of Calvary,
   Savior divine.
Now hear me while I pray;

Take all my guilt away;
O let me from this day
    Be wholly Thine!

May Thy rich grace impart
Strength to my fainting heart;
    My zeal inspire!
As Thou hast died for me,
Oh, may my love to Thee
Pure, warm, and changeless be,
    A living fire!

While life's dark maze I tread
And griefs around me spread,
    Be Thou my guide;
Bid darkness turn to day,
Wipe sorrow's tears away,
Nor let me ever stray
    From Thee aside.

When ends life's transient dream,
When death's cold, sullen stream
    Shall o'er me roll,
Blest Savior, then, in love,
Fear and distrust remove;
O bear me safe above,
    A ransomed soul!

Blessed the Hungry/ Woe to the Well Fed

Our Goals for This Session

By the power of the Spirit working through God's Word, we want to

- search out what Jesus means by "hungry" and "well fed";
- apply those terms to ourselves as His Word indicates; and
- let the Scriptures tell us how to be hungry and why to consider that hunger a blessing.

Getting Started

Have two members of your group each read one of the following scenarios.

The Hungry Village

All life moved too slowly to be real. Men sat along the road leaning against the walls of their mud hovels, peering with dry eyes across drier fields. Starvation bloated the bellies of the children. Their limbs hung from them like sticks.

Women pressed around our Jeep, begging and weeping for their children. They didn't need to convince us. We didn't doubt their need.

"We're going to have to radio headquarters," I told Hal, my assistant. "This shipment isn't going to be near enough."

Hal snorted. "This is just the first village, Jim. You haven't seen anything yet."

The Happy Hunter

Ed always felt right at home when he walked through the doors of the Happy Hunter Restaurant, especially on a winter's night like tonight. He spotted Jason, the young waiter, tossing his apron below the counter and getting ready to go home. Ed relished the thought. He'd have time to savor his meal.

His eyes scanned the menu without reading. He had memorized it by now. What shall it be? Ribs? Sliced beef? T-bone? Kansas City strip, medium rare? Or maybe some seafood as a change of pace?

The soup came—a hearty, homemade vegetable. Then the chef salad, topped high with cheeses and meats. The aroma of the hot baked and buttered bread made Ed's mouth water. Then came the three-quarter pound K.C. strip steak, so juicy it made a puddle for the baked potato. Hardly into his feast, Ed's mind was off food and on to which movie he'd watch tonight. He pulled out his newspaper and turned to the feature section. His eyes caught a splashy ad for the latest blockbuster. He chose that one, even before he chose apple pie for dessert. Soon Ed was out the door, pleasantly content.

The busboy picked up not only a hefty tip from Ed's table, but about half of his three-quarter pound steak as well. "No," the busboy told the manager with a look of shock in his eyes, "I wouldn't eat off another man's plate. This is for my dog."

In each of these scenarios, appetite played a prominent role. The characters' relationships to food spoke clearly about the characters themselves.

13. Some form of hunger is evident in each case. Just what kind of hunger (physical, emotional, spiritual) do you see in each?

14. Of the scenarios, which character(s) were:

a. Most aware of their needs? Least aware? Explain your answer.

b. Most likely to accept help? Least likely? What makes them likely or unlikely to accept help?

15. Walk through these scenes yourself, and take a quick look at each of the people. Which would you consider the most blessed? Why?

Who Is Hungry? Who Is Well Fed?

Few of us are ever hungry because we lack food. Physically, we are well fed. Then, aren't we blessed? Or are we under "woe"?

16. Some people might interpret Jesus' words to mean that only the starving people of Third World nations or inner-city communities are "blessed" in Jesus' sight. They might also believe that those who regularly have enough to eat are doomed. How would you respond to that claim?

17. Read Matthew 5:6. Here, when Jesus speaks about "those who hunger" being blessed, He helps us see more clearly just whom He's talking about.

a. In your own words, what does Jesus mean by hungering and thirsting for righteousness?

b. Considering the impact Jesus had on this crowd (see Matthew 7:28–29), He must have touched many who hungered and thirsted for righteousness. What was it about Jesus that "filled" so many of them?

18. Many people hungered for the righteousness Christ Jesus gives. Others did not. Read Luke 18:9–14. Why did this Pharisee consider himself holy? Why does Jesus consider this "well fed" condition a dangerous one (vv. 9, 14)?

19. People who hunger for righteousness do so because they know they don't have any righteousness of their own! When it comes to goodness, holiness, or being spiritual people, they're starving. And they know it!

a. Then why does Jesus consider this "hungry" condition a blessing? (See John 6:32–35.)

b. Why won't the "hungry" ever be satisfied by looking to their own resources for righteousness?

c. Describe from your own experience what it is like to hunger after righteousness. How did God answer that hunger for you?

Finding the Feeder

Divide into smaller groups of three or four. Then together dig into Matthew 5:10–11, deeper than you ever have before! Take notes based on the questions below. (Assign at least one secretary for your group.)

20. Complete the following:

a. In verse 10: Persecution will come because of

b. In verse 11: Persecution will come because of

21. The two different reasons for persecution are really the same single reason!

a. Therefore, when we hunger for righteousness, we are really hungering for:

b. How did it happen that we received this righteousness from God? (See Romans 3:21–24.)

c. How does it feel to be righteous? What makes it different than being self-righteous?

22. We know we are sinners by nature. That's why we hunger for an outside source of righteousness. So we may be shocked if we are persecuted "for righteousness' sake" (v. 10). We might say, "I don't deserve this"—not because we want to get out of persecution, but because we never thought we were enough like Christ.

a. Therefore, what exciting message is Jesus telling us in vv. 10–12?

b. Persecution is not a sign that God has abandoned us. It's the very opposite: When Christ Jesus works through us to witness in the world, the world identifies us with Jesus! Share how you think and feel about this promise.

23. In Matthew's account, Jesus refers to both "hungering" and "thirsting" after righteousness. Both eating and drinking are involved. Read John 6:54–56.

a. How can we eat and drink the righteousness of Jesus?

b. Besides giving it to us through the Word, your local congregation provides for frequent opportunities for a very special eating and drinking by which we receive this righteousness. Why is it not possible to "overeat"—or get too much of—this meal?

c. Suppose someone does not crave Holy Communion. Is this person under Jesus' "woe"?

In Conclusion

The hungry are blessed. Jesus satisfies them! Spiritual craving doesn't mean we do not know Jesus Christ. Jesus describes the life of the Christian as one constantly craving—a craving continually satisfied by Jesus Himself through His Word and Sacrament. Reflect back on "The Hungry Village" and "The Happy Hunter." As Christ's people, what could you do and/or say to the people in each scenario?

Remind each other of cherished times when you ate and drank with Jesus and with your fellow sinners.

In Closing

Close with prayer. Pray for each other, as well as for those not present who hungrily await your invitation to come to the banquet. Let them in on the blessings you already enjoy.

Prayer: Give us also our daily bread. Guard us against greed and anxiety about the body, that we may confidently rely on You for all blessings. Amen. (Martin Luther, 1483–1546)

Close by singing or reading in unison "Take My Life and Let It Be" (*LSB* 783; *ELH* 444; *CW* 469; *LW* 404; *LBW* 406; *TLH* 400).

Take my life and let it be
Consecrated, Lord, to Thee;
Take my moments and my days,
Let them flow in ceaseless praise.

Take my hands and let them move
At the impulse of Thy love;
Take my feet and let them be
Swift and beautiful for Thee.

Take my voice and let me sing
Always, only for my King;
Take my lips and let them be
Filled with messages from Thee.

Take my silver and my gold,
Not a mite would I withhold;
Take my intellect and use
Ev'ry pow'r as Thou shalt choose.

Take my will and make it Thine,
It shall be no longer mine;
Take my heart, it is Thine own,
It shall be Thy royal throne.

Take my love, my Lord, I pour
At Thy feet its treasure store;
Take myself, and I will be
Ever, only, all for Thee.

Blessed the Weeping/ Woe to the Laughing

Our Goals for This Session

By the power of the Spirit working through God's Word, we want to

- search out what our Lord means by those "who weep now" and those "who laugh now";
- discover whether or not we have applied these terms to ourselves and others according to His will; and
- attempt to let Scripture help us own both godly sorrow and godly joy.

Getting Started

Have two members of your group read the parts of Karl and his pastor:

Karl: Pastor, we've got to do something about all the unsaved people in this church. I'm getting embarrassed even to claim membership here.

Pastor: Unsaved people? What do you mean?

Karl: You know what I mean! Can't you see how they go up to Communion all glum and downcast?

Pastor: Well, I admit folks here at St. Paul's are pretty serious about worship, but glum and downcast? Do you really see it that way, Karl?

Karl: See it that way? Pastor, it is that way! People around here act as if they've been baptized in vinegar! They're so hung up on their sins. There's just not enough joy in this congregation, and it's had me upset for a long time.

Pastor: Well, perhaps . . . (*He is cut off.*)

Karl: And with all due respect, Pastor, you're not helping things much.

Pastor: Oh? Help me understand.

Karl: Well, I know you mean well, and I have as much respect for tradition as anyone. Yet if you would just let us skip that "poor, miserable sinner" part of the church service, it might help a little. How can people have a positive attitude and a negative self-image all at the same time?

Pastor: Karl, I'm sorry you feel that way. I know a lot of folks here who are very grateful for God's grace and forgiveness. Besides, you know there's always been a "downside" to being a believer. In Old Testament times, people even wore sackcloth and heaped ashes on their heads! And some early New Testament churches included loud weeping during the sermon because believers were coming to see the weightiness of their sin.

Karl: That's it! That's the word. "Weighty. "Everybody is so weighty around here. Doesn't anyone realize that "the fruit of the Spirit is . . . joy"? JOY! Come on, Pastor! Sackcloth? Martin Luther cleared all that self-punitive stuff out of the way, didn't he? The dark ages of the Church are through, Pastor. Open up the dungeons.

Karl was a very active and helpful member at St. Paul's. Yet some obvious friction developed between him and most of the congregation—including the pastor.

24. Describe the emotional condition of the folks at St. Paul's. Use specifics from both Karl and his pastor. In your opinion, how does your congregation compare? How about you personally?

25. Describe Karl's idea of what a Christian is like. How does Karl seem to feel about the Christian's attitude about sin?

26. To whom do Jesus' words "Blessed are you who weep now" (Luke 6:21b) seem most readily to apply—to Karl? to the other members of St. Paul's? Give reasons for your answer.

Who Are the Weeping? Who Are the Laughing?

Read Luke 6:21b and 25b. Those who weep are blessed? Those who laugh are under woe? That's not how we normally view things. After all, who would ever get up in the morning and say, "Thank God! I'm depressed again today!" Or who would ever say of someone, "Poor fellow, he's having a jolly time"?

Godly Sorrow

Karl and many like him hope to find joy and happiness in their church, their worship, and their lives as Christians. When Karl failed to find the joy and happiness he expected, he blamed the congregation, the pastor, and the worship style.

Yet, the Christian writer C. S. Lewis pointed out that although Christianity leads to utter happiness and joy, it does not begin there. Often it begins in sadness, despair, and even suffering.

27. What does Lewis mean, that Christianity begins in sadness? Do you agree or not? Why?

28. Read James 4:4–10.

a. James calls his readers to repentance. Repentance is going back to God (v. 8). What outward signs of repentance does James list? inward signs?

b. The apostle, in verse 9, sounds very much like Jesus in Luke 6:21b and 25b. He's actually calling for the emotional response of mourning and gloom! Why?

c. Are there times when such a call is appropriate for us in the Church today? Explain your answer.

d. Imagine that the pastor read Karl this Scripture text. What do you think would be Karl's reaction?

29. God can work through the sorrow we experience. Read 2 Corinthians 7:8–10. The apostle Paul did not enjoy see-

ing the Corinthian Christians sorrowful, but one thing about it made him happy. Reread verses 9 and 10.

To what "good" thing can godly sorrow lead? Share, only if you wish, when sorrow led you back to Christ.

30. Not all sorrows are alike (2 Corinthians 7:10–11). There is a clear difference between godly sorrow and worldly sorrow. (See Luke 21:34–36 for a description of worldly sorrow.) From the list below, which are examples of godly sorrow? worldly sorrow? Explain your reasoning.

a. Feeling sorry for yourself

b. Feeling sorrow for the hurt you caused your spouse

c. Brooding over the promotion you lost

d. Being upset because you fell to a persistent sin—again

e. Peter's tears (Luke 22:61–62)

f. Judas's rope (Matthew 27:3–10)

What invitation does Jesus offer to keep us from being weighed down by worldly sorrows (Luke 21:36)?

Godly Joy

People responded to Jesus in two distinct ways. Some rejoiced at Jesus. Others rejected Him. Read Luke 7:29–35.

31. a. John the Baptizer sang a dirge of repentance, but which group wouldn't cry, wouldn't repent? Why not?

b. Jesus played the flute of joyful freedom from the Law's accusations: the forgiveness that comes by the Gospel. Yet which group wouldn't dance? Why not? List some contemporary examples.

32. What kind of people were found in the group that rightly rejoiced in their salvation? How do you know they went through sorrow to get there? Think of specific "people" examples (see Matthew 9:9–13 or Luke 7:36–50 for starters). List some contemporary examples.

The Last Laugh

We disciples are no greater than our Master. Despite the hype of artificial Christianity, which promises happiness, good feelings, and prosperity for following Christ, our Lord lets us know we are in for the same thing He went through.

Jesus willingly suffered anguish (see Luke 22:39–46). One joy for "weepers" is that this suffering is no disgrace!

33. What did Jesus do when He was in anguish (v. 44)? Interestingly, He invited His first disciples to do the same thing (v. 46). As disciples, what comfort does this offer us?

34. Feeling low, sorrowful, or depressed is hardly a sign that God has abandoned us! We are freed from the "gotta be happy" mentality that dictates we must be high if we're really Christian.

a. Our relationship to God does not depend on our feelings. Read the very familiar text John 3:16. This time, read "love" as meaning God's constant, never-fluctuating love. How can this promise help you even when you don't feel happy?

b. "Restore to me the joy of Your salvation" (Psalm 51:12), wrote King David. Share a time when you've felt this restored joy of salvation. How might this be celebrated—in Holy Communion? in daily life?

35. Jesus had the last laugh over sorrow, sin, and death. Read Isaiah 53:11 and Hebrews 12:2–3.

a. Jesus kept the long-range view in mind. He could endure suffering and sorrow because, in the end, He would have *you*! One thing that got Him through the crucifixion was the joy of sharing *your* company forever in His Father's home. Share how this news can help you through whatever sorrow you're enduring now.

b. What friend of yours needs to hear this Good News now? How are you going to tell that friend?

Conclusion

Weepers are blessed! With Jesus they will "laugh last." Although sorrow over sin may not feel like a happy, blessed condition, Jesus' Word assures us that it is. We are freed! Freed from artificial happiness. Freed from the hyped-up message that we must always be high if our faith in Christ is genuine! We are freed because our eternal relationship to God depends not on our emotional state but on what Jesus Christ did on the cross for us.

In Closing

In your closing prayers, let each of you mention a friend who is sorrowing. Ask our Lord to give you the love and the words to help your friend see sorrow as a blessing. Ask our Lord to find a special way of telling that friend, "Blessed are you who weep now."

Prayer: Pray together Psalm 46.

Close by singing or reading in unison "O Bless the Lord, My Soul" (*LSB* 814; *ELH* 369; *CW* 238; *LW* 457; *LBW* 538; *TLH* 27).

O bless the Lord, my soul!
  Let all within me join
And aid my tongue to bless His name
  Whose favors are divine.

O bless the Lord, my soul,
   Nor let His mercies lie
Forgotten in unthankfulness
   And without praises die!

'Tis He forgives thy sins;
   'Tis He relieves thy pain;
'Tis He that heals thy sicknesses
   And makes thee young again.

He crowns thy life with love
   When ransomed from the grave;
He that redeemed my soul from hell
   Hath sov'reign pow'r to save.

He fills the poor with good;
   He gives the suff'rers rest.
The Lord hath judgments for the proud
   And justice for th' oppressed.

His wondrous works and ways
   He made by Moses known,
But sent the world His truth and grace
   By His belovèd Son.

Blessed the Despised/ Woe to the Popular

Our Goals for This Session

By the power of the Spirit working through God's Word, we want to

- examine Jesus' view of the sufferings we experience on account of our Christian faith and discipleship;
- search the Scriptures for the priorities our Lord wishes for our lives and pray for the Spirit's aid and power to apply them; and
- seek the joys Jesus promises to the faithful who endure rejection from the world.

Getting Started

Ask two members of your group to read the parts of Shelly and her mother, Caroline.

Shelly: Mom, I just can't believe how so many good things have turned so sour lately. Before, I used to be one of the "in" kids. My grades came easy. I had no trouble making cheerleader. I was employee of the month three times. I had plenty of friends, and lots of boys wanted to date me. But college has changed all that! Now I'm a reject. The girls in my dorm think I have a psychological disorder just because I'm still a virgin. Some of my professors think I'm anti-intellectual because I don't accept evolution. And my boss says he will demote me to dishwasher if I don't wear the skimpy waitress uniforms.

Caroline: Shelly, that's a mighty big load you're carrying. And as though that wasn't enough, is there something wrong between you and Eric?

Shelly: Yeah. I told him I don't want to go to any more concerts where everybody gets high. So, we had a fight. He tried to kiss and make up, but he wanted to do a lot more than just kiss. Mom, I'm starting to feel that I'm weird. Like an alien from some other planet!

Caroline: I'm awfully sorry, Shelly. No wonder you've been feeling so depressed.

Shelly: Do you think I'm taking myself too seriously? Should I just lighten up? Mom, I'm so sick of being abnormal, so different, like a stranger in my own school. Does being a Christian still mean being served as supper to lions?

Caroline: (*smiling*) It did once, I hear.

Shelly: I always thought—rather, I always used to think— that being a Christian made you a good person and would give you a good life: Do good, and good will happen to you. But it doesn't work that way, does it?

Shelly was faced with some difficult decisions. Many of her assumptions about the benefits of being a Christian were put to the test.

36. Discuss: Did you ever have an experience like Shelly's? If so, how was it similar? different?

37. Shelly worried that she brought these hurts down upon herself, that there was something wrong with her. How would you reply to that fear?

38. Shelly felt that good would be rewarded. Suppose she asked you, "What's the use of trying to do good?" How would you respond?

39. Read Luke 6:22. Do Jesus' words apply to Shelly, or is her situation not serious enough? Give reasons.

Who Are the Despised? Who Are the Popular?

Defining "the Despised"

Our culture prides itself on its tolerance. Every opinion, belief, philosophy, and religion must be regarded as good, as equal to any other. In such an open society it seems incredible that Christians could ever become objects of hatred—especially the kind of hatred Jesus predicted for His followers.

Nevertheless, we have been told from the Word that "all who desire to live a godly life in Christ Jesus will be persecuted" (2 Timothy 3:12). To examine our calling to be Christ's "blessed despised ones," carefully read Luke 6:22–23.

40. Four kinds of treatment are dealt out to Christ's people. List them on chalkboard or newsprint.

a. Which treatment do you consider the most hurtful?

b. What acts of faithfulness to God would most likely result in this kind of treatment?

41. According to Jesus' words in the Luke text, persecution does not have to be physical; it may also be psychological, social, spiritual.

a. How is persecution of Christians taking form in your country? community?

b. Share, if you are able, what persecution you may be enduring. Would this persecution cease if you were not Christ's person? Explain.

42. What causes people to persecute Christians?

43. Strangely, some persecutors are quite religious. Read John 16:1–3. Why do you think this happens?

Defining "the Popular"

In our society it's hard not to be spoken well of, since speaking well of all views, opinions, religions, and ideologies is supposed to be a sign of tolerance and intelligence.

Christians, then, are tempted to strive for popularity by tolerating what God does not tolerate. That is why Jesus' remark is especially pointed today: "Woe to you when all people speak well of you, for so their fathers did to the false prophets" (Luke 6:26).

44. How are we, as Christians, most tempted to have "all people speak well of [us]?" Share, if you can, when you've felt this temptation.

a. Describe what it's like when we fall into it and gain "people approval."

b. Describe what it's like when we resist it and face mass rejection.

45. Unlike youths, most adults are not afraid to express their opinions—unless it costs! If there are repercussions, loss of face, or sacrifice involved in carrying a belief through to an action, then we are as vulnerable to pressure as college or high school youths. Discuss the pressures you would feel in the following situations:

- Your local public school board promised to refrain from scheduling athletic events on Wednesday nights, "church night." Yet because the high school basketball team may have a chance for the state finals, the board announced tournament plays beginning on Ash Wednesday. You begin to protest, until fellow church members stress the importance of team and community spirit. They remind you that your own son is a star player and that the tournament could lead to a university scholarship.

- "Diet Dancers" want to rent your church's facilities on Thursday morning for an exercise class. The financial offer will enable your congregation to meet its mortgage payments (finally!). Yet, your congregation's largest Bible study group meets every Thursday morning. An elder suggests your Bible study group move your Bible study day.

Suggest other situations, perhaps from your own experience. Discuss how you deal with running the risk of unpopularity for the cause of Christ.

I'm Blessed Because I'm Hated?

Naturally, we want people to like us. Yet our Lord tells us that His disciples will have to forgo popularity. More than that, He tells us that we can feel good about being wrongfully treated on His account: "Rejoice . . . and leap for joy" (Luke 6:23). How is this possible?

Rejected with the Best of Them

46. Reread Luke 6:23 closely. What reason does Jesus give for rejoicing as we are mistreated?

47. Jesus compares our treatment with that of Old Testament prophets who were mistreated for their faithfulness to God. Divide the texts equally among your group:

a. 1 Kings 19:1–5

b. Daniel 3

c. Jeremiah 20:7–11

d. Hebrews 11:32–40

48. What New Testament Christians have been hated or mistreated because of their union with Christ and His Church?

49. To the degree we are hated, excluded, insulted, ignored, or persecuted because of Christian faith and actions, we become partners and teammates with the prophets and apostles. You are in their company! Share how that makes you feel. Why does Jesus say that is a reason to rejoice?

On the Coattails of Christ

While persecution joins us with the prophets and apostles, New Testament writers found even greater reason for rejoicing in rejection. So may we.

50. Read Hebrews 2:14–15. Jesus destroyed the holder of death's power. He is the winner; Satan is the loser. How do you feel about Christ inviting you to participate in the victory over Satan that He won? (See also Revelation 12:10–11.)

51. Read Philippians 3:7–10.

a. There is a fellowship among those who suffer with Christ. How does it happen that we know, and become like, Christ in our suffering?

b. Suffering may mean that we lose all earthly respect, security, and achievements; yet why is that nothing to be ashamed of?

c. Perhaps we can better see the power of Christ's resurrection at work when we suffer for Him. Explain how this might happen.

52. We actually participate with Christ in His sufferings when we innocently suffer for His cause. Read 1 Peter 4:12–16.

a. On the world's Last Day, we will get to participate in another event with Christ. What is that event (v. 13)?

b. How can this text help Shelly when she wearies of being different? How can it help you?

c. We know we will be rejoicing on that upcoming date. How does that help us begin our rejoicing now?

53. List some specific avenues of witnessing and mutual ministry that may be opened to you, even if it will involve suffering or persecution. List ways you may "crush Satan under your feet" (Romans 16:20) by means of Christ's Word, accompanied by Christian suffering.

Conclusion

Despised by the world, Christ's people are blessed. We belong to the Victor and His army of prophets, apostles, and martyrs. When hatred hurts and persecution pains, our joy is that we are in good company—that of Christ and of all who will soon celebrate the victory banquet in His Father's house.

Suppose our past is marked by timid Christianity. Suppose we feel guilt heaped on us for ducking discipleship because we panted for popularity instead.

Then it's time to start all over. Guilt is a sign to become the "poor in spirit," who need the wealth of Christ's grace. It's our chance to be "hungry," awaiting His Supper. It's our chance to "weep," awaiting the laughter of pardon and peace. You failed, and you know it?

You are blessed. Yours is the kingdom of God.

In Closing

Be sure to close with a thanksgiving for the gracious calling we have in our Baptism to be Christ's people. We may even thank God for the honor of suffering with Christ. Select someone in your group to pray for the strength and boldness to stand firm in the face of the world's hatred.

Prayer: By Your precious Holy Spirit You have also called me to Christ, my Savior, and have made me a partaker of His salvation in faith, so that I belong to that chosen generation which is Your holy nation and peculiar people in time and eternity. Graciously bestow upon me the gifts of Your Spirit, that before all the world I may show forth the praises of You who so graciously called me out of darkness into Your marvelous light. Amen. (C. M. Zorn, 1846–1928)

Close by singing or reading in unison "Rejoice, O Pilgrim Throng" (*LSB* 813; *CW* 540; *LW* 455; *LBW* 553).

Rejoice, O pilgrim throng!
　Rejoice, give thanks, and sing;
Your festal banner wave on high,
　The cross of Christ your king.

Refrain (after each stanza):
Rejoice! Rejoice! Rejoice, give thanks, and sing!

With voice as full and strong
　As ocean's surging praise,
Send forth the sturdy hymns of old,
　The psalms of ancient days.
Refrain

With all the angel choirs,
　With all the saints on earth

Pour out the strains of joy and bliss,
　　True rapture, noblest mirth.
Refrain

Yet on and onward still,
　　With hymn and chant and song,
Through gate and porch and columned aisle
　　The hallowed pathways throng.
Refrain

Still lift your standard high,
　　Still march in firm array,
As pilgrims through the darkness wend
　　Till dawns the golden day.
Refrain

At last the march shall end;
　　The wearied ones shall rest;
The pilgrims find their home at last,
　　Jerusalem the blest.
Refrain

Praise Him who reigns on high,
　　The Lord whom we adore:
The Father, Son, and Holy Ghost,
　　One God forevermore.
Refrain